C000257200

THE ECSTASY OF

COMMUNICATION

SEMIOTEXT(E) FOREIGN AGENTS SERIES

© 2012 by Semiotext(e)
Originally published in 1987 as *L'autre par lui-même* by Éditions Galilée, Paris.

All rights reserved. No part of this book may be reproduced, stored in a retrieval system, or transmitted by any means, electronic, mechanical, photo-copying, recording, or otherwise, without prior permission of the publisher.

Published by Semiotext(e)
PO Box 629, South Pasadena, CA 91031
www.semiotexte.com

Special thanks to John David Ebert, Zachary Kaplan, and Marc Lowenthal.

Cover Photography: Jean Baudrillard, *Sainte Beuve 1997.*

Back Cover Photography by Sylvère Lotringer
Design by Hedi El Kholti

ISBN: 978-1-58435-057-6
Distributed by The MIT Press, Cambridge, Mass. and London, England
Printed in the United States of America

THE ECSTASY OF COMMUNICATION

Jean Baudrillard

Introduction by Jean-Louis Violeau

Translated by Bernard Schütze and Caroline Schütze

Contents

Jean-Louis Violeau

Foreword: Baudrillard, the Ghost

The ghost is tired of hearing that it doesn't exist. It will
show them, it will show all those living people what an
appearance is when it really appears. The ghost is melan-
choly. It no longer has a good sense of where it ends and
where it begins. Is the ghost on the right or on the left? The
ghost doesn't care. It is from the beyond. The ghost despises
rotten feelings. The ghost likes emptiness, and sometimes,
the ghost has had enough of all this. But most of the time,
the ghost is amused. It leaves to humans the mirage of
believing in reality. —*Carte postale du fantôme* [Postcard
from a Ghost], Robert Malaval, painter.[1]

Yes, Baudrillard could have written this text instead of Derrida,
even if it is about a ghost. Glamor, pop and twilight: the
1980s. The end of representation, the Situationists can put their
clothes back on, they are already abandoned. Jean Baudrillard

was for sociology what Warhol was for art: a genius player, cunning, disenchanted, perspicacious and surprisingly comfortable in his element. Always one step ahead, one book ahead to finish off sociology, as others had finished off art, the perfect crime. Reversibility: the perfect counterpoint, Baudrillard ended up a photographer, fascinated with the overexposure of reality in which representation is abolished. The vertigo of simulation, he wrote in *The Ecstasy of Communication*, published by Galilée in 1987: "Everything eludes itself, everything scoffs at its own truth, seduction renders everything elusive."

Academic habilitation?

In the 1980s, *The Ecstasy of Communication*, subtitled *Habilitation*, appeared at the precise moment when the sociologist submitted a HDR—or pretended to do so. The second title, "habilitation," is important: this text was written to obtain a *Habilitation à Diriger des Recherches* [Authorization to Direct Research]. It is the crowning achievement of a French university career—for which Baudrillard could not care less. Without it, one remains a mere administrator, a lecturer for life.

To measure this distance, it is enough to recall the ironic smile with which Jacques Donzelot (well, he also remained a lecturer...) remembered his years teaching with Baudrillard at Nanterre, "the period of transition between the critical thinking of the 1960–1970s that shook up the frontiers between the disciplines and then the return to their bosom."[2] Progressively dominated by unemployment, these years saw diplomas take on renewed value as a form of reassurance while "the course that we [*Baudrillard and Donzelot*] gave stood out like a residual vacuole from a time when sociology rhymed with audacity, critique and intellectual irreverence." Sex, the social, politics? A simple rule: "I [*Donzelot*] dealt with the birth and he [*Baudrillard*] dealt with the death of each of these objects." The birth of the modern family? The dissolution of seduction. The invention of the social? The death of the social. The end of politics. The end of disciplines: "Baudrillard practices an ironic radicalness infinitely more radical than Bourdieu & Co, precisely because he undermines his academic support."

The constrained feeling of his habilitation exercise can be felt from the first page of *The Ecstasy of Communication*, at the same time as a deliberate intention to move away from it by means of irony: "pretend that this work were accomplished," writes Baudrillard, "that it developed in a coherent manner and has always existed." Quite the opposite of the applicant's position that follows in the next sentence: "I can only conceive of speaking of it in terms of simulation." The word is spoken. How can one do a retrospective panorama—the imposed form of the now canonical *Habilitation* exercise—for a body of work that has always wanted to be prospective?

Baudrillard, the sociologist? Without a doubt, but did he ever claim to speak about the world with the authority of a specific domain? The discourse of arrogance was not really Baudrillard's style, a light aristocrat, and more than one (intellectual) was irritated by it. And his Habilitation unfolded in reverse: the exercise traditionally consists of giving coherence (either real or invented) to different work, research, articles and publications accumulated over the time, most often a decade, that separates the doctoral thesis and the moment of Habilitation. Baudrillard acted clever, starting by saying that "everything started with objects, yes, *The System of Objects*, but there is no more system of objects." So be it. We have dreamed, he tells us, dreamed that the opposition between Subject and Object has been maintained, dreamed of a meaning of History, still, while History finds itself politically disinvested. The 1980s, once again.

Having held the original document in my hands, I was not dreaming: this *Habilitation* looked different in its spiral-bound version. It was more classical in style, even if it was defended at a time, in 1986, when the exercise was still new and the benchmarks still poorly defined. In the end, this habilitation was more scholarly. With a jury composed of "pillars" of the University from the time: Eugène Enriquez, but also Pierre Ansart (he passed the document to the director of my thesis who wanted to defend her own much more confidentially at the same time), Georges Balandier, Alain Touraine, all the stars! Defense held at the Sorbonne, of course.

After Baudrillard, there was no more blind spot: his master's costume did not hide any disciples. His aura did not leave anyone in the shadows. No resentment, he would have preferred it that way. Sadness of the masterless generations, smiled Deleuze. As for Foucault, he always pointed to the need for initiators of discursiveness, figures that we can refer to in order to think. Whereas Baudrillard only ever spoke of them ironically. The greatest sin of this heavy smoker? An excess of virtue. Political commitment? When he began with the review *Utopie*, definitely. Later, the forms of his commitment disappeared in his general skepticism about the world and especially his discipline: commitment, for a sociologist, most often means applying knowledge according to the rules of the academic community. And we all know the doubts, the legitimate doubts that Baudrillard regularly expressed on this subject.

Crisis

The "Crisis," our *Crisis* of principles, casts doubt on history seen as a process leading from less to more, from confusion to order, from darkness to light: a disruption of the relationship to time and especially a disruption of the relationship to the future. Prediction is a difficult exercise, especially in terms of the future! *Leave all options open* is the watchword that has become one of the categorical imperatives of late modernity with its highly misleading utopian tones. We get laid in the prospect of exorcising the lack of perspectives, remarked Baudrillard ironically in the early 1980s in the first collection of his *Cool Memories*, already under the sign of the "Crisis" reified. And this Habilitation begins with a description of the automobile of *sustainable development* that has not aged a day. It speaks to you, it is kind, its dashboard is a console, and it consoles you if needed. The car is no longer a power that you have to tame, channel or master. Ah, mastery. No, now with the car "a kind of ecological ideal is taking over, an ideal of regulation, of moderate functionality, of solidarity between all the elements of one and the same system, of the control and global management of the whole."

It's fascism, but gentle fascism. The fascism of stereotypes and artifice that are used daily and considered to be innate and natural. My dear friends, we will speak of power here, indirectly but obstinately. This is how Roland Barthes, with his characteristic elegance, began the inaugural lesson of the Chair of Literary Semiology created for him by the Collège de France in January 1977. Science is crude, life is subtle and the innocence of the Moderns, who separated power on one side and those who did not have it (yet) on the other, is definitively over. Language is worked by power: to speak is already to be subject. Language forces to speak. Signs follow the herd, and stereotypes are monsters! Baudrillard accompanies his old friend Barthes on these traces: leaders and apparatuses everywhere. Between feminine and masculine, Barthes chooses the neutral. Between subject and object, Baudrillard always voluntarily places himself beyond, in this Other by Itself and in other places later. The Subject is no longer opposed to the object. As a sociologist, the desire of the Subject always interested him less than the seduction of the object.

Jean Baudrillard did sometimes overindulge in ruptures: true style means always being the first to say "it's over." Under this regime, he is even more often than not trapped "beyond," beyond the end. The "end of" and its corollary, the "return of"… He made up for it in the year 2000, accompanying its passage under the guise of "the confederacy of dunces." And if, asked Baudrillard at the end of *The Ecstasy of Communication*, "our society were no longer that of the 'spectacle,' as was said in '68, but, cynically, that of ceremony?"

Jean-Louis Violeau, sociologist

Translated by Ames Hodges

Introduction

It is paradoxical to make a retrospective survey of a work which never intended to be prospective. It recalls the fate of Orpheus, who looked back on Eurydice too soon, and thereby condemned her to the underworld forever. One must pretend that the work preexisted to itself and forebode its own end from the very beginning. This may be an ill omen. Yet this is an exercise in simulation which may be resonant with one of the principal themes of the whole: to pretend that this work were accomplished, that it developed in a coherent manner and has always existed. Therefore I can only conceive of speaking of it in terms of simulation, much in the same manner that Borges reconstitutes a lost civilization through the fragments of a library. In other words, I can hardly examine the question of sociological verisimilitude, to which, moreover, I could only answer with the greatest of difficulty; rather I must put myself in the place of an imaginary traveler who stumbles upon these writings as upon a lost manuscript and who, for lack of supporting evidence, would attempt to reconstitute the society they describe.

1

The Ecstasy of Communication

Everything began with objects, yet there is no longer a system of objects. The critique of objects was based on signs saturated with meaning, along with their phantasies and unconscious logic as well as their prestigious differential logic. Behind this dual logic lies the anthropological dream: the dream of the object as existing beyond and above exchange and use, above and beyond equivalence; the dream of a sacrificial logic, of gift, expenditure, potlatch, "accursed share" consumption, symbolic exchange.[1]

All this still exists, and simultaneously it is disappearing. The description of this projective imaginary and symbolic universe was still the one of the object as the mirror of the subject. The opposition of the subject and the object was still significant, as was the profound imaginary of the mirror and the scene.[2] The scene of history as well as the scene of the everyday emerge in the shadow of history as it is progressively divested of politics.

Today the scene and the mirror have given way to a screen and a network. There is no longer any transcendence or depth, but only the immanent surface of operations unfolding, the smooth and functional surface of communication. In the image of television, the most beautiful prototypical object of this new era, the surrounding universe and our very bodies are becoming monitoring screens.

We no longer invest our objects with the same emotions, the same dreams of possession, loss, mourning, jealousy; the psychological dimension has been blurred, even if one can still retrieve it in the particular.

Barthes already foresaw this for the car, where the logic of possession, from the projection inherent in strong subjective relation is substituted by a logic of driving. No more power, speed, appropriation phantasies linked to the object itself, but a potential tactic linked to its use—mastery, control and command, optimization of the game of possibilities, which the automobile offers as a vector, and no longer as a psychological sanctuary—resulting in the transformation of the subject himself into a driving computer, instead of the demiurge drunk with power. The vehicle thus becomes a bubble, the dashboard a console, and the landscape all around unfolds as a television screen.

However, one can conceive of a subsequent stage to this one, where the car is still a performative instrument, the stage at which it becomes an informing network. That is, the car which speaks to you, which informs you "spontaneously" of its general state and yours (eventually refusing to function if you are not functioning well), the advising, the deliberating car, a partner in a general negotiation on lifestyles; something (or someone, since at this stage there is no more difference) to which you are *wired*, the communication with the car becoming the fundamental stake, a perpetual test of the presence of the subject vis-á-vis his objects—an uninterrupted interface.

From here on neither speed nor traveling—not even the unconscious projection, competition, or prestige—count any longer. In fact the desacralization of the car has been going on for some time now in the sense that "Speed is out! Drive more and consume less." A kind of ecological ideal is taking over, an ideal of regulation, of moderate functionality, of solidarity between all the elements of one and the same system, of the control and global management of the whole. Each system (including the domestic universe) forms a kind of ecological niche, with a relational decor where all terms must remain in perpetual contact with one another, informed as to their respective strategies and that of the entire system because the failure of one term could lead to catastrophe.

Although this is no doubt only a discourse, one must take note that the analysis of consumption in the sixties and seventies originated in the advertising discourse or in the pseudo-conceptual discourse of professionals.[3] "Consumption," the "strategy of desire" were at first only a metadiscourse, the analysis of a projective myth whose real consequences were generally unknown.[4] Actually no more was known about the relation of people to their objects than about the reality of primitive societies. This is what allows one to build the myth, but it is also the reason why it is useless to try and objectively verify these hypotheses through statistics. As we know, the discourse of advertisers is for the use of professionals in the field, and who could say that the present discourse on computer science is not accessible strictly to professionals in computer science and communication (the discourse of intellectuals and sociologists, for that matter, raises the same question).

Private telematics: each individual sees himself promoted to the controls of a hypothetical machine, isolated in a position of perfect sovereignty, at an infinite distance from his original universe; that is to say, in the same position as the astronaut in his bubble, existing in a state of weightlessness which compels the individual to remain in perpetual orbital flight and to maintain sufficient speed in zero gravity to avoid crashing into his planet of origin.

The realization of the orbital satellite in the universe of the everyday corresponds to the elevation of the domestic universe to the celestial metaphor, with the orbiting of the two-room/kitchen/bathroom unit in the last lunar model; hence to the satellisation of the real itself. The everydayness of the terrestial habitat hypostatized in space marks the end of metaphysics, and signals the beginning of the era of hyper-reality: that which was previously mentally projected, which was lived as a metaphor in the terrestial habitat is from now on projected, entirely without metaphor, into the absolute space of simulation.

Our private sphere has ceased to be the stage where the drama of the subject at odds with his objects and with his image is played out: we no longer exist as playwrights or actors but as terminals of multiple networks. Television is the most direct prefiguration of this, and yet today one's private living space is conceived of as a receiving and operating area, as a monitoring screen endowed with telematic power, that is to say, with the capacity to regulate everything by remote control. Including the work process, within the prospects of telematic work performed at home, as well as consumption, play, social relations, leisure. One could conceive of simulating leisure or vacation situations in the same way that flight is simulated for pilots.

Is this science fiction? Yes, but up until now all environmental mutations derived from an irreversible tendency towards a formal abstraction of elements and functions, to their homogenization into a single process, as well as to the displacement of gestural behaviors, of bodies, of efforts, in electric or electronic commands, to the miniaturization in time and space of processes where the stage (which is no longer a stage) becomes that of the infinitesimal memory and the screen.

This is our problem, insofar as this electronic encephalization, this miniaturization of circuits and of energy, this transistorization of the environment condemn to futility, to obsolescence and almost to obscenity, all that which once constituted the stage of our lives. We know that the simple presence of television transforms our habitat into a kind of archaic, closed-off cell, into a vestige of human relations whose survival is highly questionable. From the moment that the actors and their phantasies have ceased to haunt this stage, as soon as behavior is focused on certain operational screens or terminals, the rest appears only as some vast useless body, which has been both abandoned and condemned. The real itself appears as a large, futile, body.

The era of miniaturization, of remote control, and of a microprocessing of time, bodies, and pleasure has come. There is no longer an ideal principle of these things on a human scale. All that remains are miniaturized, concentrated and immediately available effects. This change of scale is discernable everywhere: the human body, our body, seems superfluous in its proper expanse, in the complexity and multiplicity of its organs, of its tissue and functions, because today everything is concentrated in the brain and the genetic code, which alone sum up the operational definition of being. The landscape, the immense geographical landscape seems a vast, barren body whose very expanse is unnecessary (even off the highway it is boring to cross), from the moment that all events are concentrated in the cities, which are also being reduced to several extremely miniaturized high places. And what about time, this vast leisure time we are left with, and which engulfs us like an empty terrain; an expanse rendered futile in its unfolding from the moment that the instantaneousness of communication miniaturizes our exchanges into a series of instants?

The body as a stage, the landscape as a stage, and time as a stage are slowly disappearing. The same holds true for the public space: the theatre of the social and of politics are progressively being reduced to a shapeless, multi-headed body. Advertising in its new version is no longer the baroque, utopian scenario ecstatic over objects and consumption, but rather the effect of the omnipresent visibility of corporations, trademarks, PR men, social dialogue and the virtues of communication. With the disappearance of the public place, advertising invades everything (the street, the monument, the market, the stage, language). It determines architecture and the creation of super-objects such as Beaubourg, Les Halles or La Villette[5]—which are literally advertising monuments (or anti-monuments)—not so much because they are centered on consumption, but because from the outset these monuments were meant to be a demonstration of the operation of culture, of the cultural operation of the commodity and that of the masses in movement. Today our only architecture is just that: huge screens upon which moving atoms, particles and molecules are refracted. The public stage, the public place have been replaced by a gigantic circulation, ventilation, and ephemeral connecting space.

The private space undergoes the same fate. Its disappearance parallels the diminishing of the public space. Both have ceased to be either spectacle or secret. The distinction between an interior and an exterior, which was just what characterized the domestic stage of objects and that of a symbolic space of the object has been blurred in a *double obscenity.* The most intimate operation of your life becomes the potential grazing ground of the media (non-stop television on the Loud family in the USA,[6] endless "slice of life" and "psy" shows on French TV). The entire universe also unfolds unnecessarily on your home screen. This is a microscopic pornography, pornographic because it is forced, exaggerated, just like the close-up of sexual acts in a porno film. All this destroys the stage, once preserved through a minimal distance and which was based on a secret ritual known only to its actors.

The private universe was certainly alienating, insofar as it separated one from others, from the world in which it acted as a protective enclosure, as an imaginary protector. Yet it also contained the symbolic benefit of alienation (the fact that the other exists) and that otherness can be played out for better or for worse. Thus the consumer society was lived under the sign of alienation; it was a society of the spectacle—but at least there was spectacle, and the spectacle, even if alienated, is never obscene.[7] Obscenity begins when there is no more spectacle, no more stage, no more theatre, no more illusion, when everything becomes immediately transparent, visible, exposed in the raw and inexorable light of information and communication.

We no longer partake of the drama of alienation, but are in the ecstasy of communication. And this ecstasy is obscene. Obscene is that which eliminates the gaze, the image and every representation. Obscenity is not confined to sexuality, because today there is a pornography of information and communication, a pornography of circuits and networks, of functions and objects in their legibility, availability, regulation, forced signification, capacity to perform, connection, polyvalence, their free expression...

It is no longer the obscenity of the hidden, the repressed, the obscure, but that of the visible, the all-too-visible, the more-visible-than-visible; it is the obscenity of that which no longer contains a secret and is entirely soluble in information and communication.

Marx already denounced the obscenity of the commodity, which is linked to the principle of its equivalence, to the abject principle of free circulation. The obscenity of the commodity derives from the fact that it is abstract, formal and light in comparison with the weight, opacity and substance of the object. The commodity is legible, as opposed to the object, which never quite reveals its secret, and it manifests its visible essence—its price. It is the locus of transcription of all possible objects: through it, objects communicate—the merchant form is the first great medium of the modern world. But the message which the objects deliver is radically simplified and is always the same—their exchange value. And so, deep down the message has already ceased to exist, it is the medium which imposes itself in its pure circulation. Let us call this ecstasy: the market is an ecstatic form of the circulation of goods, as prostitution and pornography are ecstatic forms of the circulation of sex.

One need only carry this analysis to its full potential to grasp what has happened to transparency and the obscenity of the universe of communication, which have long surpassed the obscenities still relative to the universe of the commodity.

Ecstasy is all functions abolished into one dimension, the dimension of communication. All events, all spaces, all memories are abolished in the sole dimension of information: this is obscene.

Hot, sexual obscenity is followed by cool communicational obscenity. The former implied a form of promiscuity, a clutter of objects accumulated in the private universe, or everything that remains unspoken and teeming in the silence of repression. However, this promiscuity is organic, visceral, carnal, while the promiscuity which reigns over the communication networks is one of a superficial saturation, an endless harassment, an extermination of interstitial space. When I pick up my telephone the marginal network hooks me up and keeps harping at me with the unbearable good will of that which seeks and claims to communicate. Deregulated radio speaks, sings, expresses itself.[8] All very well, but in terms of the medium the result is a space—that of the FM frequency—which is saturated with overlapping stations, so that what was once free by virtue of there having been space is no longer so. The word is free, but I am not; the space is so saturated, the pressure of all which wants to be heard so strong that I am no longer capable of knowing what I want.

I plunge into the negative ecstasy of radio.

There is a state particular to fascination and giddiness. It is a singular form of pleasure, perhaps, but it is aleatory and dizzying. If one goes along with Roger Caillois' classification of games—mimicry, *agôn*, *alea*, *ilinx*: games of expression, games of competition, games of chance, games of giddiness[9]—then the movement of our entire culture will lead from a disappearance of the forms of expression and competition towards an extension of the forms of chance (*alea*) and giddiness.

These no longer imply any game of the scene, the mirror, challenge or otherness; they are, rather, ecstatic, solitary, and narcissistic. Pleasure is no longer that of the scenic or aesthetic manifestation (*seductio*) but that of pure fascination, aleatory and psychotropic (*subductio*). This does not necessarily imply a negative judgement, since the forms of pleasure and perception undoubtedly undergo a profound and original mutation. We can hardly assess the consequences of such a transformation. In applying our old criteria and the reflexes of a "scenic" sensibility, we run the risk of misconstruing the irruption of this new ecstatic and obscene form in our sensorial sphere.

One thing is certain: if the scene seduced us, the obscene fascinates us. However, ecstasy is the opposite of passion. Desire, passion, seduction, or again, according to Caillois, expression and competition, are the games of the hot universe. Ecstasy, fascination, obscenity, communication (Caillois' chance and giddiness), are games of the cold and cool universe (even giddiness is cold, especially the giddiness of drugs).

In any case we will suffer from this forced extraversion of all interiority, from this forced introjection of all exteriority which is implied by the categorical imperative of communication. Perhaps in this case one should apply metaphors drawn from pathology. If hysteria was the pathology of the exacerbated staging of the subject—of the theatrical and operational conversion of the body—and if paranoia was the pathology of organization of the structuring of a rigid and jealous world—then today we have entered into a new form of schizophrenia—with the emergence of an immanent promiscuity and the perpetual interconnection of all information and communication networks. No more hysteria, or projective paranoia as such, but a state of terror which is characteristic of the schizophrenic, an over-proximity of all things, a foul promiscuity of all things which beleaguer and penetrate him, meeting with no resistance, and no halo, no aura, not even the aura of his own body protects him. In spite of himself the schizophrenic is open to everything and lives in the most extreme confusion. He is the obscene victim of the world's obscenity. The schizophrenic is not, as generally claimed, characterized by his loss of touch with reality, but by the absolute proximity to and total instantaneousness with things, this overexposure to the transparency of the world. Stripped of a stage and crossed over without the least obstacle, the schizophrenic cannot produce the limits of his very being, he can no longer produce himself as a mirror. He becomes a pure screen, a pure absorption and resorption surface of the influent networks.

2

Rituals of Transparency

The uncertainty of existing, and consequently the obsession of proving our existence, prevail over desire that is strictly sexual. If sexuality is putting our identity on the line (down to the fact of having children) then we are really no longer in a position to devote ourselves to this task, for we are too preoccupied with saving our identity to undertake anything else. What matters above everything else is proving our existence, even if that is its only meaning.

This can be seen in the recent grafitti in New York or Rio. The preceeding generation said: "I exist, my name is So and So, I live in New York." These signs were pregnant with meaning, which even if almost allegorical was that of the name. More recent grafitti is purely graphic and undecipherable. Implicitly it still says: "I exist," yet, simultaneously, "I have no name, I have no meaning, I have nothing to say." The need to speak, even if one has nothing to say, becomes more pressing when one has nothing to say, just as the will to live becomes more urgent when life has lost its meaning. As a result, sexuality is relegated to a position of secondary importance, to an already luxurious form of transcendence, of a waste of existence, while the absolute urgency is simply to verify this existence.

I recall a particular scene of a hyperrealist exhibition at Beaubourg, of flesh-colored, absolutely realistic and naked sculptures—or rather, mannequins—in unequivocal, banal positions. The instantaneousness of a body which is meaningless and which has nothing to say but simply exists, has a kind of stupefying effect upon its spectators. People's reactions were interesting. They leaned over to see something, to look at the texture of the skin, the pubic hair, everything, but there was nothing to see. Some even wanted to touch the bodies to test their reality, but of course that didn't work because everything was already there. The exhibition did not even fool the eye. When one has been visually deceived one takes pleasure in guessing, and even if there is no intent to deceive, to fool, the aesthetic and tactile pleasure produced by certain forms involves a kind of divination.

All that remains here is the extraordinary technique by which the artist erases all the signals of divination. Not even a trace of illusion remains underneath the veracity of the hair. Precisely because there is nothing to see, people approach, lean over and flair out this hallucinating hyper-resemblance, haunting in its friendliness. They lean over to see an astounding thing: *an image where there is nothing to see.*

Obscenity lies in the fact that there is nothing to see. It is not a sexual obscenity, but the obscenity of the real. The spectator does not lean over out of sexual curiosity, but to check the texture of the skin, the infinite texture of the real. Perhaps our true sexual act consists in this: *in verifying to the point of giddiness the useless objectivity of things.*

Often our erotic and pornographic imagery, this array of breasts, asses and genitalia has no other meaning but to express the useless objectivity of things. Nudity is but a desperate attempt to emphasize the existence of something. The genitalia is but a special effect. *Sexuality is but a ritual of transparency.* Where once it had to be hidden, sexuality today hides what little remains of reality, and, of course, participates in all of this disembodied passion.

Where does the fascination over these images come from? Certainly not from seduction (seduction always challenges this pornography, this useless objectivity of things). In truth we never *really* look at these images. Looking implies that the object viewed covers and uncovers itself, that it disappears at every instant, for looking involves a kind of oscillation. These images, however, are not caught in a game of emergence and disappearance. The body is already there *without even the faintest glimmer of a possible absence,* in the state of radical disillusion: the state of pure presence. In an image certain parts are visible, while others are not; visible parts render the others invisible, and a rhythm of emergence and secrecy sets in, a kind of watermark of the imaginary. While here everything is of equal visibility, everything shares the same shallow space. And fascination comes precisely from this disembodiment (Octavio Paz's aesthetic of disembodiment). Fascination is this disembodied passion of a gaze without an object, of a gaze without an image. Our media spectacles long ago crossed the threshhold of stupefaction. It is that of a vitrified exacerbation of the body, of a vitrified exacerbation of genitalia, of an empty scene where nothing takes place and which nonetheless fills our vision. It is also that of information or of the political: nothing takes place and yet we are saturated by it.

Do we desire this fascination? Do we desire this pornographic objectivity of the world? How can we know? There is without doubt a collective giddiness of escape into the obscenity of a pure and empty form, characterized simultaneously by the excessiveness of sex and its disqualification, as well as by the excessiveness and degradation of the visible. This fascination also concerns modern art, whose objective is quite literally to no longer offer itself to the gaze, to defy all seduction of the gaze. Modern art exerts only the magic of its disappearance.

However, this obscenity and this indifference do not necessarily lead to a dead point. They may again become collective values, as one can see in the rebuilding of the new rituals surrounding them; the rituals of transparency. We undoubtedly put on the act of obscenity and of pornography, just as others play the game of ideology and of bureaucracy (this is collectively true for the Eastern bloc), or the way Italian society puts on the act of confusion and terrorism. Female striptease *puts on an act* in publicity (note the naiveté of the feminist indictment of this "prostitution"). This is another ritual of transparency. Sexual liberation, omnipresent pornography, information, participation, free expression—if all this were true it would be unbearable. If all this were true we would really be living in obscenity, in the naked truth, in the insane pretension of all things to express their truth. Fortunately the destiny of things protects us, for at their culmination, as they are about to *verify* their existence, they always undo themselves and thereby plunge back into the secret.

No one can say if sex has been liberated or not, or whether the rate of sexual pleasure has increased. In sexuality, as in art, the idea of progress is absurd. However, obscenity and transparency progress ineluctably, because they no longer partake in the order of desire but in the order of the frenzy of the image. The solicitation of and voraciousness for images is increasing at an excessive rate. *Images have become our true sex object*, the object of our desire. The obscenity of our culture resides in this confusion of desire and its equivalent materialized in the image; not only for sexual desire, but in the desire for knowledge and its equivalent materialized in "information," the desire for fantasy and its equivalent materialized in the Disneylands of the world, the desire for space and its equivalent programmed into vacation itineraries, the desire for play and its equivalent programmed into private telematics. It is this promiscuity and this ubiquity of images, this viral contamination of things by images, which are the fatal characteristics of our culture. And this knows no bounds, because unlike sexed animal species protected by a kind of internal regulatory system, images cannot be prevented from proliferating indefinitely, since they do not breed organically and know neither sex nor death. And it is for this reason that they obsess us in this period of recession of sexuality and death: through images we dream of the immortality of protozoa, infinitely multiplying through contiguity in an asexual chain of progression.

In the rituals of transparence one must include the entire prosthetic and protective environments as substitutes for the natural biological defenses of the human body. We are all bubble-children, like the boy who died recently in the United States. He lived in his bubble, inside the medical surroundings of the NASA space suit, protected from all infection by the artificially immunized space; his mother caressed him through the glass with rubber gloves, as he laughed and grew up in his extraterrestrial atmosphere under the observation of science (he is the experimental brother of the wolf-child, the savage child adopted by wolves—today computers take care of the disabled child). This bubble-child is the prefiguration of the future, of total asepsis, the elimination of all germs, which are the biological form of transparency. He is the symbol of existence in a vacuum, until now exclusive to bacteria and particles in laboratories, but which will increasingly become our own: that is, to be pressed in a vacuum like records, preserved under vacuum like frozen foods, dying in a vacuum like the victims of unrelenting therapy. We will be thinking and reflecting in a vacuum, as illustrated everywhere by artificial intelligence.

The increasing cerebral capacities of machines would normally lead to a technological purification of the body. The human body will be able to rely less and less on its antibodies, and will have to be protected from the exterior. The artificial purification of all milieus, atmospheres, and environments will supplant the failing internal immune systems. If these immune systems are breaking down it is because an irreversible tendency called progress pushes the human body and spirit into relinquishing its systems of defense and self-determination, only to replace them with technical artifacts. Divested of his defenses, man becomes eminently vulnerable to science. Divested of his phantasies, he becomes eminently vulnerable to psychology. Freed of his germs, he becomes eminently vulnerable to medicine.

It would not be too farfetched to say that the extermination of mankind begins with the extermination of germs. Man, with his humors, his passions, his laughter, his genitalia, his secretions, is really nothing more than a filthy little germ disturbing the universe of transparency. Once everything will have been cleansed, once an end will have been put to all viral processes and to all social and bacilliary contamination, then only the virus of sadness will remain, in this universe of deadly cleanliness and sophistication.

Since thought is in its way a kind of network of antibodies and a natural immunity system, it too is severely threatened. Thought will be favorably replaced by a better system, a cerebro-spinal bubble, freed of all animal and metaphysical reflexes. Our very brain, our very bodies have become this bubble, this sanitized sphere, a transparent envelope in which we seek refuge, as destitute and overprotected as the unknown child condemned to artificial immunity and perpetual transfusions, condemned to die as soon as he will have kissed his mother.

To each his own bubble; that is the law today. Just as we have reached the limits of geographic space and have explored all the confines of the planet, we can only implode into a space which is reduced daily as a result of our increasing mobility made possible by airplanes and the media, to the point where all trips have already taken place; where the vaguest desire for dispersion, evasion and movement are concentrated in a fixed point, in an immobility that has ceased to be one of non-movement and has become that of a potential ubiquity, of an absolute mobility, which voids its own space by crossing it ceaselessly and without effort. Thus transparency explodes into a thousand pieces, which are like the shattered fragments of a mirror, where we catch a last glimpse of our image furtively reflected before it disappears. Like the fragments of a hologram, each piece contains the entire universe. It is also characteristic of the fractal object to be contained entirely in its minutest details. In this sense one can speak of the *fractal subject*, which—instead of transcending into a finality beyond itself—is diffracted into a multitude of identical minaturized egos, multiplying in an embryonic mode as in a biological culture, and completely saturating its environment through an infinite process of scissiparity.[1] While the fractal object is identical to each of its elementary components, the fractal subject dreams only of resembling himself in each one of his fractions. That is to say, his dream involutes below all representation towards the smallest molecular fraction of himself; a strange Narcissus, no longer dreaming of his ideal image, but of a formula to genetically reproduce himself into infinity.

Formerly we were haunted by the fear of resembling others, of losing ourselves in a crowd; afraid of conformity, and obsessed with difference. Today, we need a solution to deliver us from resembling others. All that matters now is only to resemble oneself, to find oneself everywhere, multiplied but loyal to one's personal formula; to see the same credit listings everywhere, be on all movie screens at once. Resemblance is no longer concerned with others, but rather with the individual in his vague resemblance to himself; a resemblance born of the individual's reduction to his simple elements. As a result, difference takes on another meaning. It is no longer the difference between one subject and another, but an internal, infinite differentiating of the same. Fatality today is of the order of an interior giddiness, of an explosion of the identical, of the "narcissistic" faithfulness to one's own sign and to one's own formula. One is alienated from oneself, from one's multiple clones, from all these little isomorphic "I"s...

Once each individual is contained in one hyperpotential point, the others have virtually ceased to exist. It is impossible to imagine this, just as it is futile to imagine space if one can cross it in an instant. Imagining the austral territories and everything separating you from them is futile the moment that an airplane can take you there in twenty hours. Imagining others and everything which brings you closer to them is futile the instant that "communication" can make their presence immediate. Imagining time in its length and complexity is futile the moment that any project is amenable to its immediate execution. For a primitive or a peasant, imagining that something could exist beyond his native space was impossible because they had never even had a premonition that something other could exist; this horizon was thus mentally impassable. If imagining is impossible today, it is for the reverse reason: all the horizons have already been traversed, you have already confronted all the elsewheres, and all that remains is for you to become ecstatic over (in the literal sense of the word), or to withdraw from, this inhuman extrapolation.

This withdrawal, which we know well, is that of the subject for whom the sexual and social horizons of others has disappeared, and whose mental horizon has been reduced to the manipulation of his images and screens. He has everything he needs. Why should he worry about sex and desire? It is through networks that this loss of affection for oneself and for others has come about, and it is contemporary with the desert-like form of space engendered by speed, the desert-like form of the social engendered by communication and information.[2]

There is a fractal demultiplication of the body (of sex, object, desire); seen from up close, all bodies, all faces look alike. The close-up of a face is as obscene as a sexual organ seen from up close. It *is* a sexual organ. Every image, every form, every part of the body seen from up close is a sex organ. The promiscuity of the detail, the zoom-in, takes on a sexual value. The exorbitance of the details attracts us, in addition to the ramification, the serial multiplication of each detail. The extreme opposite of seduction is the extreme promiscuity of pornography, which decomposes bodies into their slightest detail, gestures into their minutest movements. Our desire reaches out to these new kinetic, numeric, fractal, artificial and synthetic images, because they are of the lowest definition. One could almost say that through a technical excess of good will they are asexual, like porn images. However, we don't look for definition or richness of imagination in these images; we look for the giddiness of their superficiality, for the artifice of the detail, the intimacy of their technique. What we truly desire is their technical artificiality, and nothing more.

The same is true for sex. We exalt the detail of sexual acts as on a screen or under a microscope, or as a chemical or biological operation. We are looking for a reduction into partial objects and the fulfillment of desire in the technical sophistication of the body. In itself changed by sexual liberation, the body has been reduced to a division of surfaces, a proliferation of multiple objects wherein its finitude, its desirable representation, its seduction are lost. It is a metastatic body, a fractal body which can no longer hope for resurrection.

3

Metamorphosis, Metaphor, Metastasis

Where has the body of the fable gone? The body of metamorphosis, the one of a pure chain of appearances, of a
timeless and sexless fluidity of forms, the ceremonial body
brought to life by mythology, or the Peking Opera and Oriental theater, as well as by dance: a non-individual body, a dual
and fluid body—body without desire, yet capable of all metamorphoses—a body freed from the mirror of itself, yet given
over to all seduction? And what seduction is more violent
than the one of changing species, of transfiguring oneself into
the animal, the vegetable, the mineral or even the inanimate?
This movement makes us traitors to our own species, and
exposes us to the giddiness of all other species. This is the
model of amorous seduction, which also pursues the strangeness
of the other sex, and the possibility of being initiated into it
as into a different animal or vegetable species.

The power of metamorphosis is at the root of all seduction, including the most shifting forms of substitution: those

of faces, roles and masks. It is with a metamorphosis that we shroud every seduction; it is with a ceremonial that we shroud every metamorphosis. This is the law of appearances, and the body is the first object caught in this game.

The body of metamorphosis knows neither metaphor nor the operation of meaning. Meaning does not slip from one form to the other, it is the forms which slip directly from one to the other, as in dance movements or in oracular prophecies. Not a psychological body, not a sexual body, but a body freed from all subjectivity, a body recovering the animal felinity of the pure object, of pure movement, of a pure gestural transparition.

Indeed, it must pay for this fabulous capacity by renouncing desire, sex and reproduction. But this is a means for it not to die. For passing from one species to another, from one form to another is a means of *disappearing, not of dying*. To disappear is to disperse oneself in appearances. And dying doesn't do any good; one must still know how to disappear. Living doesn't do any good; one must still seduce.

The body of metamorphosis knows no symbolic order; it knows only a vertiginous succession in which the subject loses itself in ritual sequences. Nor does seduction know any symbolic order. It is only when this transfiguration of forms from one into the other comes to a halt that a symbolic order appears, that meaning is metaphorized according to the law.

Once the Great Game of the Fable, of Giddiness and of Metamorphosis has come to pass, and sexuality and desire have appeared, then only does the body become *metaphor*, a metaphoric scene of the sexual reality, with its procession of desires and repressions.

There is already an extraordinary degeneration in this: instead of being the sumptuous theater of multiple initiatory forms, of the cruelty and versatility of appearances, the locus of a phantasmagoria of species, sexes and of the diverse means of dying, the body is now but the exhibitor of a single make among all others: sexual difference and the scene of a single scenario, the unconscious sexual phantasmatic. It is no longer the fabulous surface of the inscription of dreams and divinities, it is now only the stage of phantasies and the metaphor of the subject. The ceremonial body cannot be made intelligible to a truth, be it metaphorical, of sexuality and the unconscious. (The limits of psychoanalysis lie herein: it has not paid heed to the Fable, while still claiming to make reference to it, and remains incapable of saying anything about this being of metamorphosis, vertiginous and nonetheless devoid of desire.)

The forms play with one another, exchanging one another without passing through the psychological imaginary of a subject. There the world is world; language is only one of its possible forms. The imaginary, our imaginary, is but the psychological vestige of the cruel prestige of forms and appearances. The imaginary is the diminished form of the genie's illusion and the reign of metamorphoses.

Psychological body, repressed body, neurotic body, space of phantasy, mirror of otherness, mirror of identity, the locus of the subject prey to its own image and desire: our body is no longer pagan and mythic but Christian and metaphorical— body of desire and not of the fable.

We have put it through a kind of *materialist precipitation*. The way in which we interpret our body today, instead of the divination derived from dance, the duel and stellar planets, the way in which we recount it in our unrecognized simulacrum of reality, as in individuated space of pulsion, of desire and phantasies, has led it to become the materialist precipitation of a seducing form, which carried within it a gigantic power of negation over the world, an ultra-mundane power of illusion and metamorphosis...

After the bodies of metamorphosis and metaphor follows the body of metastasis.

The metaphor was still a figure of exile, the soul's presence in relation to the body, desire in relation to its object, meaning in relation to language. But in exile one can always maintain a comfortable distance, a pathetic, dramatic, critical, aesthetic distance—the orphan-like serenity of one's own world, this is the ideal figure of the territory. Deterritorialization is no longer exile at all, and it is no more a metaphoric figure, it is a figure of metastasis; a deprivation of meaning and territory, a lobotomy of the body resulting from the turmoil of the circuits.[1] Electrocuted, lobotomized, the soul has become but a cerebral convolution. Moreover, it is probable that our learned neurologists will be able to locate the soul in the brain one day, just as they have located the linguistic function and the upright posture. Will it be found in the left or the right hemisphere?

The religious, metaphysical or philosophical definition of being has given way to an operational definition in terms of the genetic code (DNA) and cerebral organization (the informational code and billions of neurons). We are in a system where there is no more soul, no more metaphor of the body—the fable of the unconscious itself has lost most of its resonance. No narrative can come to metaphorize our presence; no transcendence can play a role in our definition; our being is exhausting itself in molecular linkings and neuronic convolutions.

This having been established, there are no more individuals, but only potential mutants. From a biological, genetic and cybernetic point of view, we are all mutants. Now, for mutants there can no longer be any Last Judgement, nor resurrection of the body, for what body will one resurrect? It will have changed formula, chromosomes, it will have been programmed according to other motor and mental variables, it will no longer have any claim on its own image.

In this sense a handicap opens up a veritable terrain of anticipation, a sort of objective experimentation on the body, the senses, the brain, in particular in its relation with computers; computers as a new, productive, immaterial and inhuman force, and the handicap as an anticipation of future work conditions in an altered, inhuman and abnormal universe. One must observe the blind playing a ball game—torball, created specifically for them—in which they display science-fiction-like behavior, adjusting themselves to each other by ear and the animal reflex, which will soon be the case for humans in a process of eyeless tactile perception and reflex adaptation, evolving in the systems as in the interior of their brain or in the convolutions of a box. Such are the blind, and in general the handicapped; mutant figures, because mutilated and hence closer to commutation, closer to this telepathic, telecommunicational universe than we others: humans all too human, condemned by our lack of disabilities to conventional forms of work.

By the force of circumstance the disabled person is a potential expert in the motor and sensorial domain. And it is not by chance that the social is aligning itself more and more with the handicapped and their operational advancement: they can become wonderful instruments precisely because of their handicap. They may precede us on the path towards mutation and dehumanization.

In this cybernetic peripeteia of the body, passions have disappeared. Or rather, they have materialized. The "anxiety molecule" has just been discovered! François Jacob writes that the pleasure center has been located, somewhere in the brain or in the spinal cord.[2] A miracle: it is immediately juxtaposed with the center of displeasure. And Jacob goes on to say that "Freud would have been pleased" (meaning: because Freud stood firm on the ambivalence of pleasure and displeasure, it would have pleased him that the anatomical juxtaposition in a sense verified this thesis). What marvelous naiveté. And where would one locate masochism, in pleasure or displeasure? And besides, to remain within the confines of Freud's logic: because their psychic affinity is total, shouldn't pleasure and displeasure, rather than being juxtaposed, be exchanged at a single point?

Enough of these scientific jests. What has become of seduction today, of passion, of this force which wrests the human being from all localization, from all objective definition; what has become of this fatality, or this superior irony of this evasive aspiration, or this alternative strategy?

Has it passed into the unconscious, into the repressed of psychoanalysis? If it still exists today it can only haunt objective reality, haunt the truth itself as its perversion, its distortion, its abnormality, its accident. Irony, if it exists, can only have passed into things. It can only have found refuge in a disobedience to behavioral norms, in the failure of programs, in covert dysfunction, in the silence at the horizon of meaning, in the rule of the hidden game, in the secret. The sublime has passed into the subliminal.

But does there still exist a subliminal aspect to things? Nothing could be less certain. Everything is exposed to transparency; that's why there is no more transcendence, that's also why neither repression nor transgression are any longer possible. One can no longer count on a revolution of the repressed (be it psychic or historical). It is the immanence that every thing is playing out. It is simply not certain if, in immanence, things will obey the objective laws which we are willing to grant them.

Transcendence has drawn its last breath. All that remains is the tension of immanence. What we must consider are the prodigious effects which are the consequence of the loss of all transcendence. Once severed from transcendence, it is not true that the world is left to pure accident, to a random distribution of things obeying only the laws of probability—this is the imaginary of a proud conscience which believes that things left unto themselves produce only their confusion. Yet immanence left to itself is not at all random. It deploys a connection of events or disconnection of events altogether unexpected, *in particular this singular form which combines connecting and disconnecting, which is that of the exponential.* The escalating power *"die steigernde Potenz"* stands in opposition to the dialectical movement *"die dialektische Aufhebung"* which is the movement of transcendence. This *Steigerung* is like a challenge offered by things, beings, and ourselves to the loss of references and their transcendence. Moreover one finds this connected/disconnected form in the mythic form of challenge and seduction, of which we know that it is not a dialectical relation, but an escalating power expressed by a potentialization of the stakes, and not at all by an equilibrium. In seduction we re-encounter this exponential form, this fatal quality whose destiny sometimes chances upon us, as it does for things when they are left to their own devices.

4

Seduction, or The Superficial Abyss

Seduction is not a theme which stands in opposition to others or puts an end to others. Seduction is what seduces, and that's that.

To begin with, almost a pun: we are told that everything relies on production—what if everything relied on seduction?

A pun is always a challenge, and in the triumphant era of production the mere allusion to seduction also assumes the role of a theoretical challenge. Challenge, and not desire, lies at the heart of seduction. Challenge is that to which one cannot avoid responding, while one can choose not to respond to desire. Desire takes you beyond all contracts, beyond the law of exchange, beyond equivalences, in a bidding which may have no end. Far more than the pleasure principle, it is challenge and seduction which draw us beyond the reality principle.

Seduction is not that which is *opposed to* production. It is that which *seduces* production—just as absence is not that which is opposed to presence, but that which seduces presence, as evil is not that which is opposed to good, but that which seduces good, as the feminine is not opposed to the masculine, but seduces the masculine. One could conceive of a theory dealing with signs, terms, and values on the basis of their seductive attraction, and not in terms of their contrast or calculated opposition. This theory would definitively shatter the specularity of the sign; a theory where everything would be played out not in terms of distinction or equivalence but in terms of a duel and reversibility. At last, a seductive theory of language...

A theory in which there would be many instances of this seductive operation, of this lightning flash of seduction melting the polar circuits of meaning. Thus, in the ancient cosmogony, the elements of water, earth, fire and air were not the distinctive elements of a system of classification, but attracting elements, seducing one another: water seduced by fire, fire seducing water. Seduction is the world's elementary dynamic. Gods and men were not separated by the moral chasm of religion: they continuously played the game of mutual seduction; the symbolic equilibrium of the world is founded on these relations of seduction and playfulness. All this has changed significantly for us, at least in appearance. For what has happened to good and evil, to the true and the false, to all these great distinctions which we need to decipher and make sense of our world? All these terms, torn asunder at the cost of unbounded energy, are ready at any moment to extinguish one another, and collapse *to our greatest joy.*

Seduction hurls them against one another, and unites them beyond meaning, in a paroxysm of intensity and charm.

Distinctive signs, full signs, never seduce us. Seduction only comes through empty, illegible, insoluble, arbitrary, fortuitous signs, which glide by lightly, modifying the index of the refraction of space. They are signs without a subject of enunciation, nor an enounced, they are pure signs in that they are neither discursive nor generate any exchange. The protagonists of seduction are neither locutor nor interlocutee, they are in a dual and antagonistic situation. As such the signs of seduction do not signify; they are of the order of the ellipse, of the short circuit, of the flash of wit (*le trait d'esprit*).

There has always been confusion between the distinctive sign and the discursive sign, the one of linguistics, and the other sign, the *mark* (*le trait*). Linguistics has always (fortunately) failed to grasp what seduces us in a poem, a story, a witticism. (Saussure sensed this in the "Anagrammes." But precisely because he was an anagrammatician at the time, and not a linguist or semiotician, he forebade the immanent reversibility of the sign, which in poetry causes language to consume itself in its detour.)[1]

Psychoanalysis has also failed to explain the seductive nature proper to neurosis, to dreams, to slips of the tongue, to madness itself, precisely because seduction is not of the order of the phantasy, of repression, nor of desire. Psychoanalysis only sees symptoms—it is the unhappy conscience of the sign.

Thus in Jensen's *Gravida*, which Freud studied and analyzed, the *mark* (*trait*) of seduction is the foot of this young girl, whose light gait stemmed from poising her foot perpendicular to the ground. This sign functions as pure seduction, as pure sign, and to relegate it to childhood or to the repressed unconscious, in order to make it the mere medium of Harold's phantasies, would be a contradiction. The sign falls from seduction into interpretation, and as a result Harold also falls from the enchanted sphere of seduction into the sphere of the real and the matrimonial. A fine example of the disenchantment of interpretation, of the misappropriation it can carry out in the name of any discipline, even psychoanalysis, on the very mark of seduction.[2]

The mark of seduction is more than a sign. Such is the gaze, whose force resides precisely in it not being an exchange, but a double moment, a double mark, immediate, undecipherable. Seduction is only made possible through this giddiness of reversibility (also present in the anagram), which cancels all depth, all in-depth operation of meaning: superficial giddiness, superficial abyss.

Surface and appearance: that is the space of seduction. Seduction as a mastering of the reign of appearances opposes power as a mastering of the universe of meaning. We gladly take flight from appearances and watch over the depth of meaning. Such is the law: every being, every thing must jealously guard its meaning and dismiss appearances as a malefaction. Seduction is damned (but that is not the least of its charms).

Under these circumstances only a few things and at rare moments attain pure appearance, and only these are seductive.

The entire strategy of seduction is to bring things to a state of pure appearance, to make them radiate and wear themselves out in the game of appearances (but the game has its rule, and its possibly rigorous ritual). We are forced to "pro-duce" things, in the literal sense of the word, because things have fallen under the yoke of meaning, into the deep wherefrom they must be extracted, and made to reappear in the order of the visible. Consequently the secret loses its meaning, and only the visible has any value for us. And yet one can conceive of a world where it suffices to seduce things or to have them seduce one another.

Everywhere one seeks to produce meaning, to make the world signify, to render it visible. We are not, however, in danger of lacking meaning; quite to the contrary, we are gorged with meaning and it is killing us. As more and more things have fallen into the abyss of meaning, they have retained less and less of the charm of appearances.

There is something secret in appearances, precisely because they do not readily lend themselves to interpretation. They remain insoluble, indecipherable. The reverse strategy of the entire modern movement is the "liberation" of meaning and the destruction of appearances. To be done with appearances is the essential occupation of revolutions. I am not expressing any reactionary nostalgia; I am merely seeking to regain a space for the secret, seduction being simply that which lets appearance circulate and move as a secret.

What could be more seductive than the secret? I have already said this of challenge and the flash of wit; in fact, all these things combined are part of the constellation of seduction. Just as seduction challenges the order of production, so the secret challenges the order of production, so the secret challenges the order of truth and knowledge.

What is in question here is not a thing kept secret, for this only overstimulates the will to knowledge, and always appears in the semblance of a truth. Yet there is nothing seductive about truth. Only the secret is seductive: the secret which circulates as the rule of the game, as an initiatory form, as a symbolic pact, which no code can resolve, no clue interpret. There is, for that matter, nothing hidden and nothing to be revealed. It cannot be stressed enough: THERE IS NEVER ANYTHING TO PRO-DUCE. In spite of all its materialist efforts, *production remains a utopia.* We can wear ourselves out in materializing things, in rendering them visible, but we will never cancel the secret. Herein really lies the paradox of a production which was mistaken about its finality, and which can therefore only exacerbate itself in a strange impotence. Even the protagonists of the secret would not know how to betray it, because it is no more than a ritual act of complicity, a sharing of the absence of truth, a sharing of appearances. In seduction we rediscover the practice of this sharing and the intense pleasure which accompanies it.

Thus in Kierkegaard's *The Diary of a Seducer,* the young girl is an enigmatic force and the process of seduction is the enigmatic resolution of this force, whose secret is never revealed. Had the secret been revealed it would have been sex, and sexuality would have been the final point of the story, had there indeed been one. *But there is none,* and in this regard psychoanalysis has deceived itself, and us. Beyond the story's ending and beyond the determination of sex and its truth, seduction remains a duel and an enigmatic resolution.

And so one can imagine that in amourous seduction the other is the locus of your secret—the other unknowingly holds that which you will never have the chance to know. The other is not (as in love) the locus of your similarity, nor the ideal type of what you are, nor the hidden ideal of what you lack. It is the locus of that which eludes you, and whereby you elude yourself and your own truth. Seduction is not the locus of desire (and thus of alienation) but of giddiness, of the eclipse, of appearance and disappearance, of the scintillation of being. It is an art of disappearing, whereas desire is always the desire for death.

The secret is never the repressed. It is never "everything you don't know and have always wanted to know about yourself and sex" (Woody Allen), it is that which no longer pertains to the order of truth. That which, saturated with itself, withdraws from itself, plunging into the secret and absorbing everything surrounding it. An immediately contagious giddiness: seduction operates through the subtle pleasure which beings and things experience in remaining secret *in their very sign*—while truth operates through the obscene drive of forcing signs to reveal everything.

Seduction does not only revolve around the fundamental rule—it *IS* the fundamental rule, and it exists only by virtue of never being uttered. Take provocation, for instance, which is the opposite and the caricature of seduction. It says: "I know that you want to be seduced, and I will seduce you." Nothing could be worse than betraying this secret rule. Nothing could be less seductive than a provocative smile or inciteful behavior, since both presuppose that one cannot be seduced naturally and that one needs to be blackmailed into it, or through a declaration of intent: "Let me seduce you..."

Seduction is not desire. It is that which plays with desire, which scoffs at desire. It is that which eclipses desire, making it appear and disappear. It brings forth appearances before desire only to hurl it back to its very end. First of all Brahma created from his own immaculate substance a goddess known by the name of Sharatuya. When he saw this glorious girl born of his own body, he fell in love with her. Sharatuya (who has a hundred forms) moved to the right to avoid his gaze, but no sooner had she done so than a head appeared on the right side of the god's body. And as Sharatuya turned to the left, passing behind him, two more heads appeared. She soared into the sky: a fifth head developed. Brahma then spoke to his daughter: "Let us give birth to all kinds of animated creatures, to men, suras and asuras." On hearing these words, Sharatuya returned to earth. Brahma married her, and they withdrew to a secret place, where they lived together for a hundred divine years...

Strategy of absence, of evasion, of metamorphosis. An unlimited possibility of substitution, of concatenation without reference. To divert, to set up decoys, which disperse evidence, which disperse the order of things and the order of the real, which disperse the order of desire, to slightly displace appearances in order to hit the empty and strategic heart of things. This is the strategy of oriental martial arts: never aim straight at your adversary or his weapon, never look at him, look to the side, to the empty point from when he rushes and hit there, at the empty center of the act, at the empty center of the weapon. So it is with Chuang Tzu's butcher: never see the ox, remove the evidence of the ox's body in order to reach the interstitial emptiness which joins the organs, and thereto bring the edge of your blade.

It is the same with desire in seduction: never take the initiative of desire, any more than the one of attack. The one who attacks first is lost; the one who desires first is lost. Never oppose one's desire to the desire of the other, but aim to the side, at the hollow spot of appearance, or trap him in his own lure. For seduction, desire does not exist any more than luck exists for the gambler. It is at most that which allows one to play: a stake. It is that which must be seduced, as everything else, as God, as the law, the truth, the unconscious, the real. All these things only exist in the brief instant when one challenges them to exist; they exist only by virtue of this challenge to which we call them, precisely through seduction, which opens the sublime abyss before them—the abyss into which they will plunge ceaselessly in a last glimmer of reality. If one reflects upon it, we exist only in the brief instant when we are seduced—by whatever moves us: an object, a face, an idea, a word, a passion.

Such is the attraction of the dark body of seduction. Things seem to follow their linear truth, their line of truth, but they reach their peak elsewhere, in the cycle of appearances. Things aspire to be straight, like light in an orthogonal space, but they all have a secret curvature. Seduction is that which follows this curvature, subtly accentuating it until things, in following their own cycle, reach the superficial abyss where they are dissolved.

Rare are those things which attain pure appearance. Nonetheless it is possible to conceive of seduction as the ineluctable dimension of each and every thing. No need to stage it as a strategy. By their own instigation, things are initiated into this fundamental rule, this superior convention, which orders a stake other than the real. We, like all systems, are eager to go beyond our own reality principle and to refract ourselves in another logic.

Thus in gambling money is *seduced*; it is deviated from the law of value and is transformed into a substance of bidding and challenge. Desire, then, becomes the stake of another game which transcends it, and in which the protagonists of desire are only extras. So even moral law can be seduced: in perversion, it enters as a tactical element in a ritual and ceremonial space—perversion makes moral law function as a pure convention, and the divine as a diabolical artifice.

The principle of reversibility, which is also the one of magic and seduction, requires that all that has been produced must be destroyed, and that which appears must disappear. We have unlearned the art of disappearance (art as such has always been a powerful lever of disappearance—power of illusion and of a denegation of the real). Saturated by the mode of production, we must return to the path of an aesthetic of disappearance.[3] Seduction is party to this: it is that which deviates, that which turns us away from the path, that which makes the real return to the great game of simulacra, which makes things appear and disappear. It could almost be the sign of an *original* reversibility of things. One could maintain *that before having been produced the world was seduced*, that it exists, as all things and ourselves, only by virtue of having been seduced. Strange precession, which hangs over all reality to this day: the world has been refuted and led astray *from the beginning*.[4] Because it has been led astray from the beginning, it is impossible that the world should ever verify or be reconciled with itself. Historical negativity is only a pious version of things. This original deviation is truly *diabolical*. The giddiness of simulation, the satanic ravishing of the excentricity of the beginning and the end opposes itself to the utopia of The Last Judgement, complemented by the one of the original baptism. Our entire moral anthropology, spanning from Christianity to Rousseau, original sin to original innocence, is false. Original sin must be replaced, not by final salvation, nor innocence, but by *original seduction*. Man is neither guilty nor innocent—he is seduced and he seduces. Whether he is guilty or innocent, this is his status as a subject—seduced and seducer, this is his destiny as an object, his objective destiny. The reader will have realized how Manichean this theory is. To evoke seduction is to further our destiny as an object. To touch upon the object is to rouse the principle of Evil.

Seduction is, therefore, ineluctable, and appearance always victorious. Of course we are witnessing a proliferation of systems of meaning and interpretation which seek to clear the path for a rational operation of the world. Interpretation is all the rage and is endowed, it seems, with a destructive violence—psychoanalysis, with its theory of desire and repression, is probably the last and most beautiful of these great systems of interpretation. At the same time it is evident that all these systems are prevented from producing anything based on truth or objectivity. Deep down everything is already there, in this evil reversal—the impossibility for all systems to be founded on truth, to break open the secret and reveal whatever it may be. *The discourse of truth is quite simply impossible.* It eludes itself. Everything eludes itself, everything scoffs at its own truth, seduction renders everything elusive.

The rage to unveil the truth, to get at the naked truth, the one which haunts all discourses of interpretation, the obscene rage to uncover the secret, is proportionate to the impossibility of ever achieving this. The more one nears truth, the more it retreats towards the omega point, and the greater becomes the rage to get at it. But this rage only bears witness to the eternity of seduction and to the impossibility of mastering it.

The present system of dissuasion and simulation succeeds in neutralizing all finalities, all referentials, all meanings, but it fails to neutralize appearances. It forcefully controls all the procedures for the production of meaning. It does not control the seduction of appearances. No interpretation can explain it, no system can abolish it. It is our last chance.

There is, in this sense, a contemporary strategy of seduction which would counter the surveillance and computer processes, the ever more sophisticated methods of biological and molecular control and retrieval of bodies, all the procedures of identification (which have replaced those of alienation), of forced identity, of detection and dissuasion.

• How does one disguise oneself?
• How does one dissimulate oneself?
• How does one parry in disguise, in silence, in the game of signs, indifference—in a strategy of appearance?

Seduction as an invention of stratagems, of the body, as a disguise for survival, as an infinite dispersion of lures, as an art of disappearance and absence, as a dissuasion which is stronger yet than that of the system.

The evil forces which it has raised against God, against morality, the forces of artifice and the Evil Demon of dissimulation and absence, of challenge and reversion, which it has always embodied and for which it has been damned: seduction can today reinvent these forces, and raise them against the terrorist seizing of truth and verification, of identification and programming which engulf us. Seduction remains the enchanted form of the accursed share.

5

From the System of Objects to

the Destiny of the Object

The essential exoticism is that of the Object for the subject.
— Victor Segalen

Simulation, the generalized passage to the code and the sign-value, was at first described in critical terms, in the light (or shadow) of a problematic of alienation. It was still the society of spectacle, and its denunciation, which was the focal point of the semiological, psychoanalytical, and sociological arguments. Subversion was still sought in the transgression of the categories of political economy: use-value, exchange-value, utility, equivalence. The referents of this transgression were to be Georges Bataille's notion of expenditure and Marcel Mauss's exchange-gift; in other words, another anthropological, anti-economistic version, which generalizes the Marxist critique of capital and commodity in a radical anthropological critique of Marx's postulates. In *Symbolic Exchange and Death* this critique went beyond political economy: it is death itself which becomes the very figure of reversibility (i.e., a reversal of all the codes and distinctive oppositions on which the dominant systems are founded: in the first place, the opposition of life and death—with the exclusion of death; that of subject and object, signifier and signified, masculine and feminine). The transgression of the code is the reversion of opposite terms, and therefore of the calculated differences through which the dominance of one term over the other is established. The "symbolic" is the figure of this reversion, and by the same token the figure of any possible revolution: "The revolution will be symbolic or will not be at all." As Saussure described in his "Anagrammes," even in the order of language, poetry is this reversibility of each term of the discourse, its ex-termination. Hence, the movement is one that counters an order of simulation; it is a system of distinctive oppositions regulating a meaning, and a movement striving to restore a symbolic order assimilated to a superior authenticity of exchanges.

This double spiral moves from *The System of Objects* to *Fatal Strategies*:[1] a spiral swerving towards a sphere of the sign, of simulacrum and simulation, a spiral of the reversibility of all signs in the shadow of seduction and death. The two paradigms are diversified in the course of this spiral without altering their antagonistic position. On the one hand: political economy, production, the code, the system, simulation. On the other hand: potlatch, expenditure, sacrifice, death, the feminine, seduction, and in the end, the fatal. However, both have undergone considerable inflection. The simulacra have passed from the second order to the third, from the dialectic of alienation to the giddiness of transparency. At the same time, after *Symbolic Exchange* and with *Seduction*[2] the dream of a transgression, of a possible subversion of codes, and the nostalgia for a symbolic order of any kind, born out of the deep of primitive societies, or of our historical alienation, has been lost. With *Seduction*, there is no longer any symbolic referent to the challenge of signs, and to the challenge through signs, no more lost object, no more recovered object, no more original desire. *The object itself takes the initiative of reversibility*, takes the initiative to seduce and lead astray. Another succession is determinant. It is no longer that of a symbolic order (which requires a subject and a discourse), but the purely arbitrary one of a rule of the game. The game of the world is the game of reversibility. It is no longer the desire of the subject, but the destiny of the object, which is at the center of the world.

In capitalist societies everything cannot be reduced to the dialectic of desire. To get back to the issue, if signs have a destination from the beginning, they must also have a destiny. And the destiny of signs is to be torn from their destination, deviated, displaced, diverted, recuperated, seduced. It is their destiny in the sense that this is what always happens to them; it is our destiny in the sense that this is what always happens to us. This is profoundly immoral. In every reversibility there is something immoral, which proceeds from a superior irony.

This is a prominent theme in all mythologies and cultures other than our own. In our systems we have given priority to the irreversibility of time, production, and history. Only that which refutes this all-too-beautiful order of the irreversibility of time, and the finality of things, can be fascinating.

Transgression is not immoral. Quite to the contrary, it reconciles the law with what it forbids; it is the dialectical game of good and evil. Reversibility is not a law; it does not establish a symbolic order, and it can't be transgressed any more than can a ceremony or the rules of a game. In reversibility time is not reconciled with its end, nor the subject with its finality. There is no Last Judgement to separate Good from Evil, and reconcile things with their essence.

Against all the pious and dialectical esotericisms, by which the subject cultivates the principle of his own end, one must raise this radical Exotericism, a reflection of the essential Exotericism of Segalen, the one of the Object for the subject.[3] As Segalen puts it: "If taste increases in terms of difference then what could be more savory than the opposition of irreducibles, the clash of eternal contrasts?" Against all interiorities, one must awaken this Externality, this exterior power which, beyond the final principle of the subject, raises the fatal reversibility of the Object. One must rouse the principle of Evil.

This is the only scale by which we can measure our present situation. By dint of meaning, information, and transparence our societies have passed beyond the limit point, that of permanent ecstasy: the ecstasy of the social (the masses), the body (obesity), sex (obscenity), violence (terror), and information (simulation). If, in fact, the era of transgression has ended, it is that things themselves have transgressed their own limits. If one can no longer reconcile things with their essence, it is because they have mocked and surpassed their own definition. They have become more social than the social (the masses), fatter than fat (obesity), more violent than the violent (terror), more sexual than sex (porn), more real than the real (simulation), more beautiful than the beautiful (fashion).

Hence, more beautiful than me you die, truer than me you die, more real than me you simulate, and more simulated than me you die... For critical theory one must therefore substitute a fatal theory, to bring this objective irony of the world to completion.

It is so much more fun to see our universe destined to fatality, which is not transcendent but immanent in our very processes, in their superfusion, in their overdrive, in their surmultiplication, immanent in our banality, which is also the indifference of things towards their own meaning, the indifference of effects towards their very causes. All this constitutes an original situation; that of an Evil Demon driven by a silent strategy. This is no longer the irony of the subject faced with an objective order, but the objective irony of things caught in their own devices—no longer the historical workings of the negative, but the workings of reduplication and the rising stakes, as one can see in the *Witz*, the equivalent of this fatal strategy for language.[4]

In the *Witz*, language makes itself more imbecile than it really is; it escapes its own dialectic and concatenation of meaning only to hurl itself into a process of delirious contiguity, into instanteousness, into pure contiguity, into pure "objectality." The evil demon of language resides in its capacity to become object, where one expects a subject and meaning. The *Witz* is the predestination of language to become non-sense from the instant it is caught in its own devices. In this there is passion, *a passion of the object*, which could very well make us rediscover an aesthetic force of the world, beyond peripeteia and subjective passions.

The banal, which Heidegger called the second fall of Man, after Original Sin, this very banal becomes prodigious. This is the fatality of the modern world, whose astounding depth raises to challenge reality itself.

Against the banal vision (conventional and religious) of the fatal, one must set up a fatal vision of the banal. It is at the extremities of this monotony, this insignificance, this indifference of our systems, that the sequences, unfoldings, and processes—which no longer proceed from cause and effect—appear; a challenge that is immanent in the very unfolding of things. This challenge is neither religious nor transcendent, and if there is a strategy here, it is no one's. It is an immanent reversion of all rational enterprises of structuration and power. As is evident in the social behavior of the masses (their silence, this excess of silence, which is not at all passive, but rather an overbid of silence and a strategy of indifference),[5] as well as in the excrescence of production, the uncontrolled fluctuation of currencies, the obese person's relationship with his body, or the monotony of our lives, which is a monotony on the *second level* (due to the *excess* of meaning, information, and visibility). Here things operate as though there were a will to challenge, as opposed to a willing servitude: a genius of indifference, which victoriously opposes itself to all enterprises of meaning and difference, but which cannot be attributed to one group, one class, or to particular individuals. Something forms a ground (*fait masse*), something engaged in a potential reversal at odds with the old dialectic of things, or rather foreign to it. This is the silent logic of excrescence, of excess, of deviation by excess, of a generalized reversibility springing from our very strategies, of our systems at the pinnacle of their efficiency.

Our all-too-beautiful strategies of history, knowledge, and power are erasing themselves. It is not because they have failed (they have, perhaps, succeeded too well) but because in their progression they reached a dead point where their energy was inverted and they devoured themselves, giving way to a pure and empty, or crazy and ecstatic, form.[6] Thus the social in its systematic extension creates fatal conditions for the social itself. The masses plunge into an ecstatic indifference, into the pornography of information, and place themselves in the heart of the system, at the blind and inert spot from which they neutralize and annul it. The masses use information in order to disappear; information uses the masses as a shroud—a marvelous ruse of our history (of the end of our history) where sociologists, politicians and massmediaticians are dumbfounded.

Through the sophistication of its methodology, science annihilates its object: to survive, science is forced to artificially reproduce the object as a model of simulation. Again the object takes revenge in that it exists only as a simulation in the grip of our technology. Everywhere it seems that the subject has simultaneously lost its gyroscope and its referentials, as well as the control over things, and faces a reversion of its powers where it once counted on their continuity.

The Object and the world let themselves be surprised for an instant (a brief instant in the general cosmology) by the subject and science, but today they are violently reasserting themselves and taking revenge (like the crystal!). Such is the figure of our fatality, that of an objective turnaround, of an objective reversal of the world.

The term "fatal" has nothing fatalistic or apocalyptic about it. What is implied by this term is this metamorphosis of effects (and no longer a metaphysics of causes), in a universe which is neither deterministic nor aleatory, but destined to a succession of a higher necessity. This higher necessity brings things to a point of no return, in a spiral which is no longer that of their production, but of their disappearance. That which is linked outside of the subject, that which is on the side of the subject's disappearance, is fatal. All that which is no longer a human strategy becomes a fatal strategy by that very token. Yet there is nothing transcendent about this fatality, nor can it be invoked from the outside.

The fatal is always an anticipation of the end in the beginning, a precession of the end whose effect is to topple the system of cause and effect. It is a temptation to pass to the other side of the end, to go beyond this horizon, to deny this perpetually future state of things. The Object, then, is always already a *fait accompli*. It is without finitude and without desire, for it has already reached its end. In a way, it is transfinite. The object is therefore inaccessible to the subject's knowledge, since there can be no knowledge of that which already has complete meaning, and more than its meaning, and of which there can be no utopia, for it has already been created. This is what makes the Object a perpetual enigma for the subject. This is what makes it fatal.

If the complexity of the universe were only hidden to our knowledge, it would end up by being resolved. However, if the universe is a challenge to the successive solutions offered, even the most subtle of hypotheses have no chance. Because it refines itself to infinity, the universe is reversed in accord with science. Adapting itself through a superior ruse, it reacts like a virus to antibiotics, all the while maintaining its virulence. Our knowledge would do well to revise its objectives in terms of this supple and antagonistic strategy. Yet, it is hopeless, because if science has fostered a vision of the world in terms of problems that are temporarily unsolved, the world itself resists all solutions. Even at such a cost it accepts, ironically as it were, to conform itself to the hypotheses.

Yet, is the emergence of a necessity other than the human, of a strategy overcoming the human and the subject, not a mystery? How does one explain the ironic fatality of the object, which has become indecipherable under the pressure of our procedures of control and analysis? Is there any point in waging on the geniality of the Object, or is this "fatal strategy" only a blind bid of the subject, a negation of the real, a plunge into artificial ecstasy? How could the subject dream of leaping over its own shadow, and of sinking into the perfect silence and destiny of stones, beasts, masks, and stars? It cannot rid itself of language, of desire, or of its own image, because the object only exists in that it is designated and desired by the subject.

One thing is for certain: if it is absurd for the subject to become object, then it is equally inconsequent to dream that the object can become subject. This is, however, what is maintained by the science and conscience of the Western world. Everybody wants to believe that the world becomes subject and the subject becomes the world. Even though this subjectivity is, strictly speaking, unthinkable. Even though the world is *marvelously objective* in a sense that is exactly opposed to that of materialism and science. The subject itself is marvelously objective, i.e., it cannot be alienated. Is it not its own fable, which it is telling through language and the mirror of alienation? If nothing has finality, everything is metamorphosis, everything is its own fable. There is no other meaning to the "destiny of the Object."

There is a radical convergence and divergence between these two extremes: from the object as system to the Object as destiny, from the object as structure, as structural sign, to the

Object as a pure sign, as "crystal." It was already the obsession of objects in their everyday configuration to pass through the subject, to reverse the dialectic of subject and object. If the approach was one of a critical structuralism, called for by the spirit of the times, then the wresting of objects from their current determinations (use, exchange, function, equivalence, projection, identification, alienation) was already a means of crossing to the other side of the mirror. But, after all, the object is still called upon to signify. It is the passive term of the investigation; it is neither a destiny nor a challenge, and in this situation the best the object can do is hide, as we have told it to do.

The crystal is altogether different. It is the pure Object, the pure event, which doesn't exactly have a beginning or end, and now, perhaps, begins to tell its tale. Maybe now, after centuries of willing servitude, it may even begin to take revenge? Everything is being reversed into the enigma of an Object, endowed with passions and original strategies, an object in which one senses the evil genius, a genius more evil and more genial deep down than the subject, whose endeavors it victoriously opposes in a kind of endless duel.

Let us imagine the Object in a passionate form. For the subject does not have the monopoly of passion—in fact its reserved domain would more likely be that of action. The Object is passive in the sense that it is the locus of an objec-tive, seductive and vengeful passion. This world, which we have far more often sought to interpret and transform rather than seduce, seeks perhaps to seduce us, and this seduction, as in the human reign, entails intelligence, cunning, defiance, and vengeance. If this has been concealed to us until now, it is because the subject has made the world into the metaphor of its own passions. It colonized everything: the bestial, mineral, astral, historical, and mental. But the object is not metaphor, it is passion, pure and simple. And the subject is perhaps only a mirror where objective passions come to be reflected and played out.

If the object seduces us, it is initially through its indifference. The subject passionately desires to become free, autonomous, responsible, different. The Object, however, has the passion of indifference. The passions of the subject are differential, energetic, ethical and heroic passions. Indifferential, inertial passions are those of the Object. The ironic passions of cunning, silence, conformity, and willing servitude are opposed to passions of liberty, desire, transgression, the passions of the subject. Implosive passions versus explosive passions. Yet above all the subject has *the passion to be object*, to become object—an enigmatic desire, whose consequences we have barely evaluated in all domains, whether political, aesthetic, or sexual, lost as we are in the illusion of the subject, its will and its representation.

The crystal takes revenge.

The sphere of the soul's passions, the major concern of psychology and fiction for two or three centuries, has considerably diminished. The sphere of "drives," which has only been the major concern for fifty years, also seems threatened. What is left? Of all possible movements of the soul, only two apparently contradictory ones seem to remain: indifference and impatience. They oppose the traditional qualities of the soul. Indifference opposes the soul's passionate ambition towards attaining transcendence, while impatience opposes the traditional "patience of the soul," this virtue put to the test by the world. Actually, these are no longer passions of the soul, subjective passions. There is no longer a subject of indifference or impatience. These are objective passions.

The world is becoming indifferent, and the more indifferent it becomes, the closer it seems to move towards a superhuman event, an exceptional ending reflected in our increasing impatience. Not only we, but history and events seem to be prey to the combined effects of impatience and indifference.

It is not I who is indifferent or impatient. The world itself seems to want to hurry, to exacerbate itself, losing patience with the slowness of things, and at the same time it sinks into indifference. It is no longer we who give the world meaning in transcending or reflecting upon it. The indifference of the world in this respect is marvelous; marvelous is the indifference of things in respect to us, and yet things passionately unfold and confuse their appearances. (The Stoics had already expressed all this with great eloquence.)

6

Why Theory?

It is here that language and theory alter their meaning. Instead of acting as a mode of production, they act as a mode of disappearance, just as the Object has become the subject's mode of disappearance. This enigmatic game is no longer that of analysis; it seeks to preserve the enigma of the object through the enigma of discourse.

To be the reflection of the real, to enter into a relation of critical negativity with the real, cannot be theory's end. This was the pious vow of a perpetuated era of Enlightenment, and to this day it determines the moral standing of the intellectual. Today, however, this appealing dialectic seems unsettled. What good is theory? If the world is hardly compatible with the concept of the real which we impose upon it, the function of theory is certainly not to reconcile it, but on the contrary, to seduce, to wrest things from their condition, to force them into an over-existence which is incompatible with that of the real. Theory pays dearly for this in a prophetic autodestruction.

Even if it speaks of surpassing the economic, theory itself could not be an economy of discourse. It must become excessive and sacrificial to speak about excess and sacrifice. It must become simulation if it speaks about simulation, and deploy the same strategy as its object. If it speaks about seduction, theory must become seducer, and deploy the same stratagems. If it no longer aspires to a discourse of truth, theory must assume the form of a world from which truth has withdrawn. And thus it becomes its very object.

The status of theory could not be anything but a challenge to the real. Or rather, their relation is one of a respective challenge. For the real itself is without doubt only a challenge to theory. It is not an objective state of things, but a radical limit of analysis beyond which nothing any longer obeys the real, or about which nothing more can be said. But theory is also made solely to disobey the real, of which it is the inaccessible limit. The impossibility of reconciling theory with the real is a consequence of the impossibility of reconciling the subject with it own ends. All attempts at reconciliation are illusory and doomed to failure.

It is not enough for theory to describe and analyse, it must itself be an event in the universe it describes. In order to do this theory must partake of and become the acceleration of this logic. It must tear itself from all referents and take pride only in the future. Theory must operate on time at the cost of a deliberate distortion of present reality. In this one must follow the model of history, which has separated many things from their nature and mythical origin in order to reverse them in time. Today they must be wrested from their history and their end to recapture their enigma, their reversible path, their destiny.

Theory itself must anticipate its own destiny, because for every thought one must expect a strange tomorrow. Theory is, at any rate, destined to be diverted, deviated, and manipulated. It would be better for theory to divert itself, than to be diverted from itself. If it aspires to any *effets de vérité* it must eclipse them through its own movement. This is why writing exists. If thought does not anticipate this deviation in its own writing, the world will do so through vulgarization, the spectacle or repetition. If truth does not dissimulate itself, the world will conjure it away by diverse means, by a kind of objective irony, or vengeance.

Once again, what is the point of saying that the world *is* ecstatic, that it *is* ironic, that the world *is* objective? It is those things, that's that. What is the point of saying that it is not? It is so anyway. What is the point of not saying it at all? What theory can do is to defy the world to be more: more objective, more ironic, more seductive, more real or more unreal, what else? It has meaning only in terms of this exorcism. The distance theory takes is not that of retreat, but that of exorcism. It thus takes on the power of a fatal sign, even more inexorable than reality, and which can perhaps protect us from this inexorable reality, this objectivity, from this brilliance of the world, whose indifference would enrage us if we were lucid.

Let us be Stoics: if the world is fatal, let us be more fatal than it. If it is indifferent, let us be more indifferent. We must conquer the world and seduce it through an indifference that is at least equal to the world's.

To counter the acceleration of networks and circuits the world will seek slowness, inertia. In the same movement, however, it will seek something more rapid than communication: the challenge, the duel. On the one side, inertia and silence. On the other, challenge and the duel. The fatal, the obscene, the reversible, the symbolic, are not concepts, since nothing distinguishes the hypotheses from the assertion. The enunciation of the fatal is also fatal, or it is not at all. In this sense it is indeed a discourse where truth has withdrawn (just as one pulls a chair out from under a person about to sit down).

Conclusion

And what if reality dissolved before our very eyes? Not into nothingness, but into the more real than real (the triumph of simulacra)? What if the modern universe of communication, of hyper-communication, had plunged us, not into the senseless, but into a tremendous saturation of meaning entirely consumed by its success—without the game, the secret, or distance? If all publicity were the apology, not of a product, but of publicity? If information no longer had anything to do with an event, but were concerned with promoting information itself as the event? If history were only an accumulative instantaneous memory without a past? If our society were no longer that of the "spectacle," as was said in '68, but, cynically, that of ceremony? If politics were increasingly a dated continent, replaced by the dizziness of terrorism, of a generalized hostage-taking, this very figure of the impossible exchange? If all this mutation did not arise out of a manipulation of subjects and opinions, as some believed, but out of a logic without a subject, a logic in which opinion has collapsed into fascination? If pornography signified the end of the sexual as such, from the instant that sex in its obscene form has invaded everything? If seduction followed desire and love, that is, once again the reign of the object and that of the subject? If, as a result, strategy replaced psychology? If it were no longer a question of setting truth against illusion, but of perceiving the prevalent illusion as truer than truth? If no other behavior were possible but to learn, ironically, to disappear? If there were no more fractures, no more vanishing lines, no more lines of rupture, but only a surface that is full and continuous, surface without depth, without interruption? And if all this were neither exciting, nor despairing—but fatal?

Notes

Foreword: Baudrillard, the Ghost

1. March 2011, this text by Robert Malaval (1937–1980) was read by his grand-daughter Edween on stage at the Maison des Arts de Créteil (MAC) where, over several days in 1980, Maraval threw his glitter-dusted energy onto the canvas while warning spectators, *Attention à la peinture, exposition pirate!* [Watch out for the painting, pirate exhibit!] Thirty years later, the event was put on stage by Jean-Charles de Castelbajac.

2. Jacques Donzelot published this text under the title "Patasociology at the University of Nanterre" (pp. 59–66) in the *Cahier de L'Herne* dedicated to *Baudrillard* in 2005 under the direction of François L'Yvonnet.

1. The Ecstasy of Communication

1. These concepts derive from Marcel Mauss and Georges Bataille, and were used extensively in Baudrillard's *L'Échange symbolique et la mort* (Paris: Gallimard, 976), translated as *Symbolic Exchange and Death* (London: Sage Publications, 1993).

2. A reference to Jacques Lacan's celebrated "mirror phase," developed in *Écrits* (New York: Norton, 1977), and explored in Baudrillard's own *Le Miroir de la production* (Paris: Casterman, 1973), translated as *The Mirror of Production* (St. Louis: Telos Press, 1975).

3. See Jean Baudrillard's *La Société de consommation* (Paris: Denoël, 1970), translated as *The Consumer Society* (London: Sage Publications, 1998).

4. An allusion to Gilles Deleuze and Félix Guattari's *Anti-Oedipus* (New York: Viking, 1977).

5. Three vast Parisian areas turned into public malls or museums. See Baudrillard's "The Beaubourg Effect," in *October* 20, (Spring, 1982).

6. See Jean Baudrillard, *Simulations* (New York: Semiotext(e), 1983).

7. See Guy Debord's Situationist manifesto, *La société du spectacle* (Paris: Buchet-Chastel, 1967), translated as *The Society of the Spectacle* (Detroit: Black and Red, 1977).

8. *Radios libres*: There was a vast political attempt to reclaim the media by means of the radio at the end of the 1970s.

9. Roger Caillois, *Les Jeux et les Hommes* (Paris: Gallimard, 1958), translated as *Man, Play and Games* (New York: The Free Press, 1961).

2. Rituals of Transparency

1. *Scissiparity* and, earlier, asexual reproduction, are concepts developed in this context by Georges Bataille; see *L'Érotisme* (Paris: Éditions de minuit, 1957), translated as *Erotism* (San Francisco: City Lights, 1986).

2. See Jean Baudrillard, *À l'ombre des majorités silencieuses* (Paris: Utopie, 1978), translated as *In the Shadow of the Silent Majorities* (New York: Semiotext(e), 1983).

3. Metamorphosis, Metaphor, Metastasis

1. A concept introduced by Gilles Deleuze and Félix Guattari in *Anti-Oedipus*, along with the process of metamorphosis.

2. François Jacob is a well-known French biologist and winner of the Nobel Prize for Medicine in 1965. See *The Possible and the Actual* (Seattle: University of Washington Press, 1982).

4. Seduction, or The Superficial Abyss

1. See Jean Starobinski, *Les Mots sous les mots* (Paris: Gallimard, 1971), translated as *Words upon Words* (New Haven: Yale University Press, 1979), and "Saussure's Anagrammes," in *Semiotext(e)* 3 (1975).

2. See Sylvère Lotringer, "The Fiction of Analysis," in *Semiotext(e)* 6 (1977) and "The Dance of Signs," in *Semiotext(e)* 7 (1978).

3. See Paul Virilio, *Ésthétique de la disparition* (Paris: Editions Ballard, 1980), translated as *The Aesthetics of Disappearance* (New York: Semiotext(e), 1988).

4. See Jean Baudrillard, *Simulations.*

5. From the System of Objects to the Destiny of the Object

1. See Jean Baudrillard, *Le Système des objets* (Paris: Gallimard, 1966), translated as *The System of Objects* (London: Verso Books, 1996), and *Les Stratégies Fatales* (Paris: Éditions Grasset, 1983), translated as *Fatal Strategies* (New York: Semiotext(e), 1988).

2. See Jean Baudrillard, *De la Séduction* (Paris: Éditions Galileé, 1979), translated as *Seduction* (New York: St. Martin's Press, 1990).

3. See Victor Segalen, *Stèles* (1912), translated as *Steles* (Middletown: Wesleyan University Press, 2007).

4. Sigmund Freud, *Jokes and Their Relation to the Unconscious* (New York: Norton, 1963).

5. See Jean Baudrillard, *In the Shadow of the Silent Majorities.*

6. See Jean Baudrillard, *Oublier Foucault* (Paris: Éditions Galilée, 1977), translated as *Forget Foucault* (New York: Semiotext(e), 1987).